LIVING WITH
AIR PLANTS

A Beginner's Guide to Growing and Displaying *Tillandsia*

PROTOLEAF
Yoshiharu Kashima

BROCANTE
Yukihiro Matsuda
STYLING DIRECTION

TUTTLE Publishing
Tokyo | Rutland, Vermont | Singapore

Contents

Part 1
Cultivating Air Plants

Part 2
The Fun of Displaying Your Air Plants

Part 3
Air Plant Reference Guide

Author's Note

At the Tokyo garden shops where I work (Protoleaf Garden Island Tamagawa branch and Tukuriba Green Chofu branch) the number of customers looking for air plants is increasing to an overwhelming degree.

Back in the day, customers were mainly enthusiasts seeking rare varieties, but these days, air plants are easy to find at nurseries, big chain stores, supermarkets, home improvement stores and so on, and are attracting more and more fans seeking a bit of versatile greenery.

In the past, it was erroneously believed that air plants require no attention, probably leading to some unsuccessful attempts at growing them.

It's true that air plants are resilient to dry conditions and are easy to cultivate, so they generally require less effort than other plants. Still, they do have their own needs. For example, although they love water, they don't do well in damp environments. Additionally, air plants come in many different forms and each variety is suited to a slightly different environment. They will thrive if cultivated in a way suited to their variety.

So to have real success with air plants, it helps to acquire some knowledge and a bit of experience with them.

In this book we will cover how to cultivate air plants and provide you with a reference guide on the particular properties of each variety. Part of the fun of having air plants is that you can display them as they are, given that they do not need soil. Yukihiro Matsuda, from the popular variety store Brocante, shows us how to bring out their charm. Their subtle colors fit into any interior and they complement succulents and other plants, so their unique appeal is sure to keep on growing.

Discovering life with your favorite air plants is a thrill—I hope you enjoy the ride.

— PROTOLEAF Yoshiharu Kashima

The Characteristics and Charm of Air Plants

As long as care is taken with watering, ventilation and sunlight, air plants (*Tillandsia*) will grow. Since they don't need to be planted in soil, they make a unique piece of interior greenery and can be moved around like an ornament. Let's take a look at the characteristic hardiness and ease of cultivation that make them so appealing.

Water is absorbed through the leaves

Air plants belong to the genus *Tillandsia* in the Bromeliad family and are native mainly to South and Central America, with around 600 original strains worldwide. In their natural habitat, most air plants attach themselves to rocks, trees and plants such as cacti and grow by absorbing moisture from rain and fog. Their main characteristic is their ability to take in moisture through their leaves, aided by organs on the leaf surface called trichomes. For this reason, they can grow even if not planted in soil.

Hardy plants resilient in dry conditions

Air plants' natural habitat varies from arid and alpine regions with little rainfall through to areas of rainforest. Essentially, they are able to live in harsh environments due to their ability to withstand dehydration and they rarely dry out. In fact, they are not appreciated in their places of origin and are treated as weeds. (It's said that the first time they entered Japan it was not as plants, but as packing material.) And these plants are generally as hardy as weeds, with significant capacity to adapt to their environment.

Ideal as indoor greenery

As air plants can be cultivated without being planted in a pot or container, there is no need to worry about soil choices, care or mess. They are ideally suited as interior objects and indoor greenery. They can be simply placed on a tray or a shelf, wound around architraves to decorate walls, hung from railings and so on to be enjoyed for the dimension they create. Of course, watering and ventilation are essential, but if their various requirements are met, they are easily cultivated with no need for fuss. They complement ornamental plants, succulents, dried flower arrangements and so on, so try displaying them together.

A variety of unique forms

The appeal of air plants lies also in their unique form and appearance. They come in various forms, with some having leaves that curl irregularly at the tips, others that open out into attractive rosette shapes and others resembling round burrs. Their leaves range from thin needle-like types to those like prickly grass, with others as soft as felt. Varying in size from dwarf plants as small as an index finger or that can fit on the palm of your hand through to giant, eye-catching types, some of their appeal lies in the pleasure that can be had in finding the best place to cultivate and display each plant to best show off its individualities.

Terms Used for Parts of Air Plants

The way that air plants flower, their leaf color, shape and so on vary depending on their type, but here we use the typical form of the *Tillandsia* geminiflora to explain the main parts of an air plant.

Leaves

The rigidity, texture and other qualities of leaves vary depending on the type of plant. Leaf surfaces are covered with organs called trichomes which absorb water, and depending on their form, number and so on, leaves appear green or silver. Some varieties of air plant take on color during their blooming period (the time at which they produce new stock, also known as pups).

Flowers

Typically, flowers can be enjoyed for around two to three weeks after blooming, with some lasting as long as a month. Some types bloom in spring or fall as the seasons turn and the amount of sunlight changes, while others are stimulated by high temperatures and bloom in summer. Flower colors include pink, red, yellow, purple and so on, with few white flowers. There are also some scented types.

Roots

The roots serve to attach the plant to trees, rocks and so on as well as to take in water and nutrients. In stores, some plants are sold without roots, but they will develop them as the plant grows.

A plant which has put out roots. If kept in place with bark chips, tree fern slabs and so on, the plant will take root well.

Flower stems

These stems produce flowers, becoming erect during the blooming period. Some flower stems are long, others divide out into several stems and others are quite short.

Part 1

Cultivating Air Plants

Air plants can be enjoyed inside as low-maintenance indoor greenery, but by nature they prefer an outdoor environment where air circulates well. And although they are sturdy and tolerate dry conditions well, they love water. Because they are hardy and don't require soil, it's easy to misunderstand and forget about their basic needs, but if properly cared for you will be able to enjoy them for a long time. Firstly, learn about their key characteristics and appropriate environments to get the knack of cultivating them. This knowledge will help when you want to enjoy displaying them indoors.

Main Types of Air Plants

Plants are divided by silver and green leaf color

Leaf surfaces are covered with organs called trichomes that aid in the absorption of water. Leaf color differs depending on the form and number of trichomes, broadly dividing into silver foliage and green foliage types. Some types are difficult to classify clearly, but the amount of water and sunlight a plant needs can roughly be determined by this division, so it is useful as a reference when cultivating air plants.

Plants with silver foliage grow relatively slowly, while green-leaved plants' growth is more vigorous. Further, because of the forms they resemble, some are known as pot types while others are grass types. Types that have the capacity to store water are called tank types.

Silver-leaved Types

Gardneri, a variety representative of the silver-leaved type. Trichomes cover the leaves to the tips and underside surfaces, making them appear white.

The length, form and other aspects of the trichomes differ depending on the plant variety. The *gardneri* in the photo has fine, velvety trichomes.

Slow growers resilient to dry conditions

Trichomes cover the entire surface of the leaves, making this type appear white to silver in color. They have an excellent capacity for moisture absorption so many are relatively resistant to dryness. Furthermore, their relatively slow metabolism and slow growth means that, in comparison with the green-leaved types, they have a tolerance for shade and do not become weak even if left in a slightly dark environment. Conversely, as they easily absorb water, their weak point is that they are prone to moldering, so it is necessary to create a well ventilated environment for them. If keeping them indoors for any length of time, avoid using terrariums and other airtight containers and ensure that they are positioned somewhere with good air flow.

Green-leaved Types

A close-up of a *capitata*. The trichomes on the surface of the leaves are barely visible (left). *Ionantha*. The area around the base of the plant is whitish but the ends of the leaves are green. As long as the plant is not covered in trichomes, it can be considered to be a green-leaved type (right).

Placed in a bright spot, they will thrive

With trichomes that are not immediately obvious, the leaves of this type appear completely green. Many plants of this type grow naturally in regions with high rainfall and will thrive if given plenty of water.

As these plants grow more vigorously than silver-leaved types, they are recommended if you are looking for fast growers. They are less tolerant of shade than the silver-leaved types and favor bright places, but be careful not to place them in direct sunlight as their leaves will burn. They are relatively resistant to steamy conditions so it is possible to display them in areas where air remains still, such as terrariums. Even if the outer edge of the leaves at the base of the plant appear silver, if the inner section is green, they should be handled as green-leaved types.

Capitata is a good example of a green-leaved type. It is characterized by its glossy green color.

- -

Classification by form

Pot shape

This refers to plants which have a bulbous base and resemble a pot. Water collects readily in the base and can cause rot to set in, so hang the plant upside down after watering to get rid of excess water. The plant in the photo is *seleriana*, with other types including *caput-medusae*, *puruinosa*, *bulbosa* and so on.

Grass types

These types have fine, straight leaves like plants in the grass family. Many of them dry out easily, so make sure they get plenty of water. The plant in the photo is *juncea*, with other types including *fuchsii*, *andreana*, *filifolia* and so on.

Tank type

This type stands out even among the *tillandsia* for its water-storing structure. Its leaves are fleshy and easily broken and it is top-heavy, so most plants of this type are sold planted in pots and it is recommended to keep them in pots to cultivate them. When watering, make sure water that has collected in the base of the plant is refreshed by pouring water in liberally. The plant in the photo is *Neoregelia chlororostica*.

11

Preferred Environments for Air Plants

Air plants like well-ventilated semi-shaded spots

Air plants grow naturally in a wide variety of regions from the southern parts of North America to the West Indies and South America. From misty mountain regions to dry desert zones and hot and humid rainforests, the environments in which they grow vary, but essentially they like places where they can receive dappled sunlight and good air flow and take in water and moisture. Apart from the winter in areas where the season is harsh, somewhere outdoors where air circulates well makes the ideal environment for cultivating air plants. If cultivating them indoors, it's important to create as similar an environment to this as possible.

1 Sunlight

Place in gentle sunlight

In their natural habitats, most air plants attach themselves to trees and so on, so they like places where they can receive soft light like that filtered through leaves. If placed outside, somewhere that does not receive direct sunlight but gets filtered semi shade, such as under the eaves, is appropriate. Indoors, somewhere that gets soft sunlight like that filtered through lace curtains is recommended, as for ornamental plants. They will not grow in places where the light is blocked out through shade curtains.

Avoid direct sunlight in summer

In spring, fall and winter, it is not a problem for air plants to receive relatively strong sunlight, but in summer, if curtains are left open and plants receive extreme amounts of direct sunlight, they can weaken from the heat and their leaves can be burned, so take care to avoid this. Basically, most varieties like light, but some can grow even in places with low levels of light.

2 Ventilation

Position them to catch a natural breeze

Ventilation is equally as important as sunlight. Air plants are more easily acclimatized to an indoor environment than succulents and can be enjoyed indoors for a long time, but most of the time if they do not thrive, it is due to ventilation. Air plants do not like water collecting on their leaves for any length of time, and ideally the water should evaporate within half a day after watering. There is no need to worry if the plants are outdoors where they can receive a breeze, but if cultivating them indoors, make sure to open the window once a day for more than 30 minutes to refresh the air and let them get a natural breeze (see p20). If ventilation is poor, make up for it by placing the plants outside for a while after displaying them indoors. If you are away for a few days, it is recommended that you put them outside before you leave.

3 Water

They love water!

Although air plants cope well with dry conditions, they are actually water-loving plants. As they absorb moisture through their leaves and the rest of their structures, some types can go for a long time without being watered, but from spring to fall, use a mist bottle or watering can once a day to water them until they are dripping wet. From spring to fall, dusk through until night is the best time for watering. In their natural habitats, night dew and night fog raise the humidity level from evening through to morning, so air plants have pores that open at night to absorb the moisture. Furthermore, it's fine to have them out in the rain, but during winter, any water that collects overnight can get cold and damage the plants, so it's best to water them once or twice a week in the morning instead. If keeping them in a dry, warm room, water them at least twice a week.

The Growth Cycle of Air Plants

Slow growers that form "pups"

The main period of growth for air plants is spring through to fall, with their development slowing as temperatures drop. Air plants grow considerably slower than other garden plants, taking anywhere between one to two years to several years for a small plant to reach maturity.

Once flowers bud and new plants, or pups, have formed, it is time for the new generation to take over. After flowering and transferring its nutrients to the pups, the parent plant's role is over and life continues with the next generation. If you want the plants to grow quickly, attaching them to tree fern slabs, driftwood and so on so that they put out roots (see p23) is an effective method.

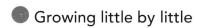 At the time of purchase

Look for a plant with a shape that is filled out all over and with fresh looking leaves (see p18). Most plants available in stores don't have roots, but this is not a problem.

 Growing little by little

Plants grow extremely slowly, taking about a year to increase in size. Spring until early summer is their growth period, with development slowing in the heat of midsummer and starting again from the end of summer through to fall. When temperatures drop from late fall to winter, growth slows.

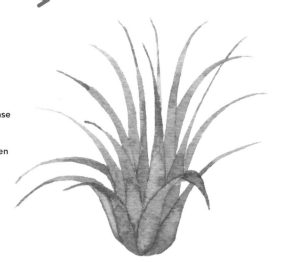

● Flowers bloom

For varieties that grow quickly, it takes about one to two years until they are stimulated to bud by the change in seasons (the change in levels of light), high temperatures and so on. The main blooming season is spring through to fall. Some types take an extremely long time to flower, with differences between varieties and even individual plants. In most cases, parent plants flower only once in their lives.

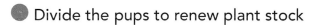

● Pups form

Usually, when flower buds form, one to two pups will also form. In many varieties, pups form at the base of the original stock plant, but some types form pups at the base of flower stems (see p22) or both on the original plant and the flower stem. In favorable environments where the plant is particularly strong and healthy, it may form pups before flowering or may form pups multiple times.

pup

● Divide the pups to renew plant stock

Once the pup has developed to about a third of the size of the parent plant, it is a signal that it has received enough nutrients, so remove it from the parent plant (see p22).

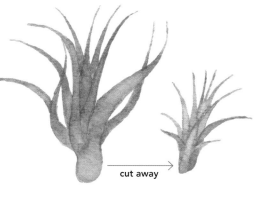

cut away

● The parent plant withers

Having transferred nutrients to the pup, the parent plant becomes weaker and weaker. As its role is fulfilled, over three to six months it turns from yellow to brown and its time for display ends. In some varieties like the *duratii*, the parent plant remains unchanged in form and can still be enjoyed for up to two years, while other varieties retain enough strength to flower multiple times.

How to Cultivate Air Plants

 Equipment and components you will need

Essential items
•••••••••••••••••••

Once you have purchased an air plant, the very first equipment you will need is for watering.

1 Spray bottle

This is used daily for watering and is handy when you only have a few plants (see p20).

2 Watering can

Used when cultivating plants outdoors. This is recommended when you have a lot of plants.

3 Bucket

Used when air plants have dried out and other times when they need to be soaked in water for a long period (see p20).

Handy items
•••••••••••••••••

These items are handy for creating attractive indoor displays and for day to day maintenance.

1 Wire

Used to attach air plants to boards, hang them from high places and so on.

2 Ornamental stones

These come in a variety of sizes. Strew them on a tray or use them to line a terrarium to set off air plants to good effect.

3 Sphagnum moss

This is sphagnum moss that has been dehydrated. It aerates and retains moisture well. Plants can be placed directly onto it or it can be secured to driftwood and so on to form cushioning. Dried fern moss offers better drainage and is also recommended.

4 Tweezers

Used for removing dead leaves and arranging details.

5 Scissors

Used for trimming off broken leaves and flowers.

Items to encourage root growth

These items help attach a plant to objects, securing roots and speeding growth as roots absorb moisture and nutrients (see p23).

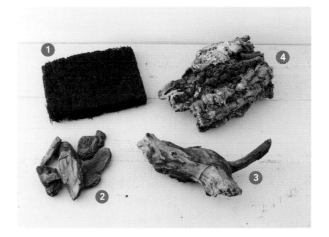

❶ Tree fern slab

This is a board or pole made from the trunk of tree ferns where the roots meet. It offers good aeration and does not molder easily.

❷ Bark chips

These are chips made from the bark of trees such as pine. They come in various sizes.

❸ Driftwood

This can be used to evoke an air of wildness. Choose a small piece for a natural effect.

❹ Cork

This is made from the bark of the cork oak. Its surface is covered in fine indentations, making it a material to which roots can easily attach.

Essential items for potted air plants

Some air plants that like water are suited to potting. Tank types can be cultivated in pots.

❶ Pots

Both pottery and plastic types are OK, but if the pot is too large, the plant's roots will rot, so choose the size that matches the plant at the time of purchase and repot in larger containers as the plant grows.

❷ Bark chips (small) and pumice chips

Mix equal parts of bark chips and pumice chips to create soil which drains well but retains a good amount of water. It's fine to use potting media for Western orchids too.

Items not suitable for use with air plants

Regular potting mix for flowering plants drains too well so is not appropriate for air plants as rot can set in from the roots which are in contact with the soil. Coconut fiber is light and aerates well, but has the disadvantage that once it is damp, it doesn't dry out well. Additionally, its fibers are long, creating large areas of contact with the air plant and making aeration difficult.

Tips on selecting plants and varieties

Choose a plant that has taken in plenty of water and is nicely filled out. A healthy plant that is properly hydrated is springy to the touch, has a glossy look and has some weight to it when held in the hand. Look for a well-formed plant with leaves in the center that are full of life. Avoid plants with withered leaves or whose form has deteriorated.

While air plants come in a wealth of varieties, the ones listed in the air plant reference guide are recommended as they are generally easy to come by and easy even for beginners to cultivate. Bear in mind that there's no guarantee as to what varieties will be available to you, so be sure to explore your local sources. You're sure to find types that appeal to you.

The plant has an overall plumpness and is well hydrated. The plant in the photo is a *paucifolia*.

The outer leaves have not had enough light and have opened out considerably, but the new shoots at the center have a good glossy color to them. The plant in the photo is an *ionantha*.

The new shoots are standing straight and tall and there are a lot of leaves in the center. The plant in the photo is an *andreana*.

A plant with burnt leaves and that is withered overall is not such a good choice. The plant in the photo is an *ixioides*.

 # What to do after purchasing a plant

After purchasing an air plant, it is enough just to water it. There is no need to do anything such as repot it as you would for other plants. Using p20 as a guide, have a spray bottle or watering can on hand and give the plant plenty of water. Not having a spray bottle doesn't mean you can roughly water the plant using water directly from the faucet, as a strong flow of water will ruin the fine hairlike trichomes that cover the leaf surfaces.

The tank types that are available in pots do not need particular care after purchase either. If repotting them, April to May is the ideal time to do so.

Locating air plants to suit the season

As mentioned in Preferred environments for air plants (see p12-13), air plants favor places that are well ventilated and receive good amounts of sunlight. Here, we cover appropriate locations and points to keep in mind depending on the season.

 ## Spring Fall

This is the time of year when plants' metabolism and growth are at their best. They do not damage easily and it is the ideal time to enjoy them indoors as interior greenery. Make sure to give them plenty of water.

The amount of sunlight needed differs depending on the variety, but even if they have the capacity to tolerate dark places well, they essentially do not like them, so make sure to place them somewhere bright. At this time of year, even if plants receive strong sunlight, it will not immediately damage them.

If the area is well ventilated, a plant placed directly on a cabinet, tray and so on will have no problems growing, but it is a good idea to place it on a net or something else that will stop

it directly touching a surface, thereby preventing dampness. Hanging plants from the ceiling is a good way to prevent them from moldering. Air plants favor similar conditions to ornamental plants, so cultivating them together by hanging air plants from the branches of ornamental plants, or winding them around the branches, is an idea to consider.

If cultivating air plants in an enclosed space, it is important to give them outdoor air regularly, for example by placing them outside for a while if they are not healthy. If the maximum temperature outdoors reaches above 86F/30C degrees, move them to a cool spot or into the shade. There is no problem if they receive rain.

Summer

Heat-loving air plants should love summer, but this is true only when they have proper ventilation. Air plants are particularly vulnerable in muggy or humid conditions. Left in an extremely hot, enclosed room, they can become damaged within even only one day. It's the season to give up displaying them indoors—consider it a time for them to rest.

If you are away from home during the day, it's safest to place them somewhere outside that is cool and out of the sun, such as under the eaves in a north-facing spot. Strong sun will weaken the plant and result in burnt leaves so must be avoided. If keeping them on a porch or veranda, put up a reed screen to create shade and hang them from the clothesline as you would hang your washing. Avoid placing them close to air conditioning sources or vents as the air is too drying.

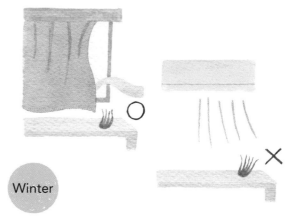

Winter

This is the season when the temperature drops and growth slows. Once the minimum temperature gets to below 44-47F/7-8C degrees, bring in any air plants that were being kept outside and place them somewhere that they can receive filtered sunlight such as that through a lace curtain. They will not wilt immediately if left outside but should definitely not be allowed to get wet in the rain.

Even if kept indoors, care must be taken not to place plants directly in the line of warm air from heat sources as they will dry out too much. If the air is too dry, use a humidifier or place plants on a layer of sphagnum moss; or if growing them on a board, dampen the wood to create moisture around the plants. Also, make sure they get some natural breeze by refreshing the air during the warmest time of each day.

Xerographica, *streptophylla* and other types which need a minimum of 50F/10C degrees over winter will rot if they get too cold, so after watering, hang them upside down to make sure water doesn't collect in their centers.

Watering

From spring to fall, water once a day in the evening using a spray bottle or watering can. If using a spray bottle, give it about 10 pumps until the plant is dripping to make sure it gets enough water. Spray both the front and back surfaces of the leaves, then turn the plant upside down and shake off excess water. This is necessary because if water is left in the spaces between the leaves, it can heat up in summer and boil the plant, while in winter, it can get too cold and may cause the plant to rot.

Ideally, plants watered in the evening should be dry on the surface the next morning. If it takes time for them to dry, reduce watering frequency to once every two to three days and monitor their condition. It is not good for the plants' surfaces to be left wet for more than 15 hours.

Air plants open their pores from evening to morning, so will absorb water well if watered in the evening, but in winter it gets too cold so they should be watered in the morning instead. It is fine to water only once a week in winter, increasing the frequency accordingly depending on how dry the plant gets.

It's easiest to water outdoors or at a sink. Hold the plant in your hand and spray water firstly into the center of the leaves until droplets form and start to drip from the plant. Spray the back surfaces and base of the plant too. Once the plant has had plenty of water, turn it upside down and shake it a few times to shed any excess.

Emergency Soaking

Soaking is a method of watering which involves placing plants in a bucket full of water to let them absorb it. It is an emergency measure for plants that have become dehydrated and is not necessary if plants are properly watered every day. Make use of it when you have been away or otherwise unable to water for a while and your plants have withered and collapsed. Leave the plants in the water for around 5-6 hours before removing them. In the winter, if the water is too cold, plants may suffocate, so check on them and adjust conditions accordingly. If plants are attached to driftwood or other items, soak the entire arrangement.

Use a bucket big enough to hold water to submerge plants entirely. For plants with leaves that are easily bent or for large plants, soak them individually, making sure the leaves are not damaged.

Refreshing the air

Air plants do not cope well with stuffy conditions, so if cultivating them indoors, ideally a window should be left open at all times. In reality this isn't always possible, so refresh the air for about half an hour once a day. The natural breeze entering the room has an appropriate amount of moisture, so this is ideal for plants. If plants are positioned somewhere with bad ventilation, make sure to put them outside on a regular basis to keep them healthy. Plants that have deteriorated due to being kept in an enclosed space can be revived by being placed outdoors out of direct sunlight for at least a week.

Fertilizer

Air plants can be cultivated well even without fertilizer, but it is effective in improving the luster of leaves, the growth rate and so on.

If you want to fertilize air plants, use a liquid fertilizer meant for ornamental plants and dilute it to one part in 1000, then apply to the plant using a spray bottle. As a rule of thumb, apply once monthly from April to October during the growth period. It is not necessary during winter.

Applying fertilizer should only be done when the plant is plump and thriving. If it is showing signs of weakness or dehydration it should be avoided. Fertilizing too often can burn the plant, so make sure not to be overzealous.

After flowering

Air plants do not put out flower buds until they reach maturity. For this reason, some may flower within a year, while others may not bloom for several years.

The flowering period is irregular but often occurs in spring and fall, with flowers lasting from between two weeks to a month. Flowers are mainly red, yellow, pink or purple in color and very flamboyant. If you want to admire the flowers for a while, there's no need to prune them off right away, but blooming uses up the plant's energy, so if you prefer to prioritize the development of the pups that form at the same time as the flowers, trim off the flower stems early.

Some types have flower stems that grow long and form pups along their lengths, so for those types, wait until the pups have formed before trimming.

Some types like the *puruinosa* in the photograph gain color when flower buds form (see p70 for the plant's usual color).

Pups form around the same time as flowers bud. After blooming, the parent plant transfers nutrients to the pup, withering and dying within about half a year.

Use scissors to trim the dead flowers off at the base of the flower stem. The plant in the photo is a *stricta* which has grown in a clump. The number of flowers a *stricta* has differs from plant to plant.

Tips for flower lovers

There is some difference between varieties as to how easy it is to get them to bloom, so choose a variety that flowers readily. *Ionantha*, *stricta*, *bulbosa*, *aeranthos* and *geminiflora* (pictured) are all recommended. Plants flower depending on their environment, the maturity of the plant and so on, so there is no particular method to ensure flowering, but some may bloom earlier if they are cultivated in plenty of sunlight, although not so much that their leaves burn.

Dividing the stock

As air plants form pups, the parent plant withers and dies, so at the appropriate time, the pups should be removed to form new stock.

If the pup is separated from the parent plant when it is too small, it won't have received enough nutrients, so gently remove it when it is about a third of the size of the parent plant.

1

A *brachycaulos* with a pup forming at its base

2

Hold the plant firmly but gently to remove the pup from the parent plant. Stock can be divided at any time regardless of the season.

3

The parent plant (left) and pup (right). Parent plants usually die within half a year to a year of flowering, but some plants may have the strength after flowering to form pups multiple times.

Most air plants form pups at their base, but depending on the variety some types form pups at the base of their flower stems. Pictured is a *stricta*.

Dividing clumps

Some varieties of air plant form several pups at once. When many pups stem from the plant this is called a clump. Clumps are popular but are prone to moldering so for them to develop properly it is safest to divide them. If you want to enjoy plants in clump form, use tweezers or scissors to remove the withered leaves of the parent plant in the center which may otherwise create stuffy, smothering conditions, and place the clump in a well ventilated spot.

Plants in clump form. Pictured is a *bergeri*.

 # Protecting against pests

They don't do a lot of damage, but watch out for spider mites, scale insects and the like. Both of these pests tend to increase if the plant has dried out from lack of proper watering. Scale insects tend to infest the spaces between leaves and the bases of the leaves. Spider mites suck the plant's sap, leaving unattractive black spots all over the leaves that are particularly noticeable on plants such as *brachycaulos* and *capitata*. Regular watering and maintaining the appropriate level of humidity helps keep pests at bay.

Cultivating roots for better growth

Air plants can grow even if simply placed on a piece of pumice or bark chips, but if you recreate the ecology of their natural environment where they attach themselves to trees and so on, they will take root more readily and grow more quickly. Plants that are secured to bark chips, tree fern slabs, driftwood and so on will start putting out roots in about three months.

1 Use a drill to make holes in the wooden platform (such as the bark chip pictured) through which wire can be passed. Bark chips are hard and split easily, so enlarge the hole a little at a time.

2 Remove withered leaves and growth from the plant and wrap sphagnum moss around its base. The moss forms cushioning to prevent the plant being damaged by the wire.

3 Wrap wire around the sphagnum moss to secure it to the plant.

4 Pass the wire through the hole in the wood to secure the plant to the platform. Bits of the sphagnum moss will fall off, but they can be replaced later.

5 The underside of the wooden platform. Wind the wire firmly around it to make sure the plant can't be shifted.

6 The completed arrangement. After a while the roots of the air plant will attach to the surface of the bark chip. Use a spray bottle to water the entire arrangement including the roots.

Types that can be potted

Most tank types (see p11) are sold in pots and can be cultivated as they are. Furthermore, some types that are sold with their roots already growing can develop more quickly if potted (these are listed in the air plant reference guide from p54-93). If you are potting an air plant, follow the steps on the right to pot it for the first time. The process is the same if repotting. It is best to pot or repot plants from April to May.

1 To prevent moldering, make only a shallow planting. As a rule of thumb, cover the plant with soil only below the dotted line in the photo.

2 Mix pumice stone and bark chips in a 1:1 ratio to form soil and place plant in it (see p17). Repot plant once a year to prevent roots from becoming choked.

Watching for warning signs
What do I do if...? Q & A

We want to enjoy our air plants in peak condition, and sometimes we may worry that they are not at their best if leaves are damaged and the plant seems to be losing strength. Listed here are some common questions about air plants' health and their remedies.

A plant with broken leaves. Use scissors to remove the damaged sections if they are bothering you.

Q *The tips of the leaves are broken and damaged. Is it all right to leave them like this?*

A *It's fine to leave them as they are, but if they are bothering you, use scissors to trim them off.*

Air plants' leaves are often broken off or damaged on the surface due to contact with other plants and so on, but from a growth perspective this does not present a problem. If their appearance bothers you, trim off the damaged sections with scissors. If a type with a stem snaps in two, it is unlikely that both the stock plant and the split section will wither. However, in giant varieties like the *duratii* (p70) the section that has lost its growing point will die away, but pups may emerge from the broken section.

Q *The outer sections of the plant have gone completely brown. Does this mean it is dying?*

A *Even if the outer sections are slightly withered, if the center of the plant is green, it is alive.*

Types that grow in a rosette shape and those with stems, among others, grow by shedding their lower leaves or those in the outer layers, in the same way as succulents. Even if the outer leaves are dying away, as long as the leaves in the center and near the growing point are green and vibrant, the plant is fine. However, it makes the plant look unattractive, so use scissors to trim off dead leaves at their base. This also prevents moldering.

The stem of this *latifolia caulescent* form has grown long. Trim off withered leaves at their base with scissors. Soft leaves can be removed by hand.

A dried-out *brachycaulos* (left) and a well hydrated example of the same variety (right).

Q *The leaves are curling inwards. What can I do?*

A *This is a sign of dehydration and can be remedied by soaking the plant.*

Depending on the variety, the leaves of some air plants curl inwards naturally, but if they are curling in more than when the plant was purchased it is a sign of dehydration. If the leaves look like those in the picture on the left, it is a sure sign that the plant has dried out. A plant like this feels light when you pick it up and looks crumpled and obviously lacking in moisture. The remedy for this is to soak the plant as per the instructions on p20. If doing this in winter, check the condition of the plant to make sure it is not damaged by the cold.

Q *The trichomes of my* tectorum *look a bit dirty. How do I get them back to their original light, fluffy state?*

A *Some varieties with a lot of trichomes do better with less water.*

Tectorum (see p66) grow naturally in arid regions and in order to absorb small amounts of moisture extremely efficiently, their trichomes have developed to be long and as fine as baby's hair. This light, fluffy hair is also the secret to their popularity. However, if conscientiously watered, the role of the trichomes is diminished and emerging buds will have fewer, shorter trichomes. To remedy this situation, reduce the frequency of watering. Essentially, even among silver-leaved types with many trichomes, it is only the *tectorum* that may be affected by this phenomenon, as most varieties like water. Observe plants regularly to alter care accordingly.

A plant whose trichomes have become shorter (left) and one with fluffy trichomes (right).

Q *The center part of my* xerographica *has completely detached. Is there a way to help the plant recover?*

A *Unfortunately once the growing point is damaged the plant can not recover.*

Air plants such as *xerographica* (p60) that are structured so that water collects easily at their centers (near their growing points) should be turned upside down and shaken after watering to get rid of excess water. Neglecting to do this may result in the center section becoming too moist and overheated or rotting due to becoming too cold from the pooled water. If the leaves at the center of the plant feel wobbly, it will be very difficult to restore the plant to health. The most effective measure is to make sure to shake off excess water whenever watering the plant. Take care with varieties such as *streptophylla* (p64), *seleriana* (p66) and others which have dense, layered foliage or form pot-like shapes which collect water easily.

Q *The leaves have started turning black. What is causing this?*

A *This discoloration is due to moldering. Move the plant to somewhere with good ventilation.*

Moldering causes leaves to turn black. This tends to happen if the plant is left in an enclosed space for a length of time, such as when you are away on vacation. Particular care is needed during summer, when humidity levels rise. If the green parts at the center of the plant are still firm and strong the plant will recover, so place it outside immediately in a well-ventilated spot and leave it there for a while. The discolored sections will not regain their original color, so encourage new growth for the plant's recovery. Continue watering as usual.

More About Air Plants

❶ Air plants in their homelands and their popularity in other parts of the world

As mentioned on p6, air plants are looked on as weeds in their countries of origin. They spread as easily as as dandelions, chickweed and goose grass do other regions, and can be seen everywhere, so they are not particularly appreciated. Elsewhere, though, apart from Spanish Moss (*usneoides*, p57), air plants have come to be used in displays in stores such as fashion and gift shops and are now a familiar sight.

Air plants have become popular in the US, Europe, Japan, China and Korea. In Japan, they experienced their first wave of popularity more than 10 years ago. Unfortunately at that time the appropriate ways to care for them were not communicated and many people lost their plants due to mistakenly believing that they did not require watering. Now that their care needs are more widely known and unusual varieties have increased in availability, their popularity as indoor greenery is thriving in Japan and other parts of the world. Light and simple to hang for display, air plants make handy dimensional decorations for walls and other spaces.

In their native habitats, many air plants attach themselves to trees and other objects, securing themselves with their few roots. Pictured is an *ionantha*.

❷ Their curves show they are growing towards the sun

When shopping for air plants, you may see some that are curved in < or U shapes. Most of the plants that grow in < form are growing towards the sun; this occurs frequently in caulescent types (types with stems).

Plants mainly grow in U shapes when they have started trailing towards the ground and then change direction. Air plants that have grown relatively straight and then been hung with their growing point facing down form a U as their growing point aims in an upwards direction.

An aff.duratii that has formed U shapes.

Giant varieties such as *duratii* (p70) have particularly dynamically growing stems. One theory behind this is that in their native habitat, they needed to receive sunlight and breeze efficiently and developed the ability to bend their stems and leaves so as to best entwine themselves around trees.

If you want to bring out the unique aspects of air plants, make use of these characteristics and consider them when deciding how to display the plants.

❸ Various names of air plants

As some varieties may be relatively new imports to certain parts of the world, their official names may not be universally established among nurseries worldwide. For this reason, air plants may be sold with their variety name followed by their country of origin and "xx form" which describes their defining shape, thereby creating a name that allows the plant to be easily visualized.

Even if the plant is from a major variety, sometimes plants with unusual characteristics enter the market, so if you see a plant with a long name, ask the shop staff what kind it is.

These days, there are seemingly endless opportunities for buying air plants online. This has pros and cons—it makes the plants easier to obtain, but you can't judge their quality before you buy. Be aware that some vendors, particularly those selling starter kits and assortments, may not name any or all of the plants in the package. If you want something specific, you'll need to search for it by name. It's a good idea to check reviews of any vendor you use, to minimize the chances of receiving poor quality plants.

Part 2

The Fun of Displaying Your Air Plants

Here, we share some ideas for displaying air plants which, as they need no soil, present a lot of creative options. We include lots of tips on how to enjoy air plant arrangements that complement spaces such as entrance halls and dining rooms. You're free to combine any varieties that you like, but check the air plant reference guide (p54–93) for how to care for them. This information will help when you want to enjoy displaying them indoors.

An Entrance Hall Where Small Air Plants Offer Greetings

Here, we've hung air plants alongside a hat, stole and other bits and pieces. Joined by linen cord, these small plants are a charming accessory, and even the tiniest of them will capture attention. Matched with natural materials and dried flora, this arrangement keeps the space fresh.

● Materials and equipment

Air plants (nine, of six different varieties)
linen cord
wire
radio pliers

● Method

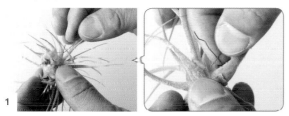

1

Pass wire through leaves close to their base, winding around the plant. Once the wire has gone around the plant, twist it to hold in place.

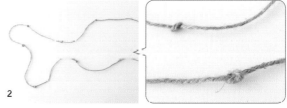

2

Prepare a length of linen cord and make knots along it, keeping in mind the overall balance and only making as many knots as there are air plants.

3

To secure air plants, pass one end of the wire wound around the plant through a knot in the cord and twist both ends of wire together.

4

Attach each air plant to the linen cord, considering the plant variety, size and so on as well as the overall balance as you go.

● Air plants used

A *Scaposa*
B *Veluntina*
C *Ionantha*
D *Magnusiana*
E *Bulbosa*
F *Fuchsii fuchsii*

● Display and care

Try displaying this arrangement in a bright entrance hall lit by a small window. The idea of joining plants together on a linen cord is not only visually interesting, it also makes it easy to move the arrangement. Ease of watering and airing is also a feature of this idea. If plants end up upside down when hung, this presents no problem to their development. The dry appearance created by the leaf color and texture makes this a good match for items such as dried flowers.

A Windowside Mobile That Sways in the Slightest Breeze

Strong, bold leaves stretch from these air plants.
Hung in mid-air, don't they look like wild birds freely fluttering around?
Swaying ever so slightly, the glass pieces in this air plant mobile occasionally catch the light,
spreading a peaceful feeling through the room.

● Materials and equipment

Air plants (seven, of six different varieties)
Mobile with glass pieces
Wire
Radio pliers

NOTE: This mobile is a great way to display air plants with natural light. You can make an attractive mobile from hemp or wire and any pre-drilled glass with finished edges. Drilled capiz shells also enhance light beautifully.

● Method

1

2

Choose air plants of a size that will be easy to hang and place them on the pieces of glass on the mobile to check the overall balance.

Wind wire around the air plants and pass the ends through the hole in the glass pieces, twisting to secure.

● Air plants used

A *Stricta*
B *Exserta*
C *Capitata*
D *Bulbosa*
E *Schiedeana*
F *Mima chiletensis*

● Display and care

For humidity-hating air plants, somewhere mid-air where they can catch the breeze is ideal. A swaying mobile will mean happy air plants. Display them in a bright room close to a window. Hanging them like this will make them prone to drying out, just as laundry dries when hung, so water them a little more often than usual. Use a spray bottle to water them as they are, making sure to lightly shake off excess water.

Adding an Urban Flavor to a Wall

....

It seems that in their native lands, *usneioides* often can be seen hanging from telephone poles, signs and so on. Air plants seem to complement shabby bits and pieces on street corners. This wall lettering that looks like it could be used in a neon sign conjures up the image of a city in the American South, one of air plants' native habitats.

● Materials and equipment

Air plants (12, of 10 different varieties)
Sphagnum moss

● Method

1

2

Place moistened sphagnum moss where you want to display the air plant and position the air plant on top. The surface of the moss is stable and makes it easier to cultivate the air plant.

Pat down lightly to ensure the air plant takes to the moss.

● Air plants used

A *Xerographica*
B *Ionantha* Ron
C *Capitata Red*
D *Ionantha Rubra*
E Tricolor
F *Cacticola*
G *Brachycaulos*
H *Capitata*
I *Usneoides*
J *Schiedeana minor*

● Display and care

Make sure the sphagnum moss is well hydrated. It's fine to display the air plants without putting down the moss first, but wrapping them with sphagnum moss and securing it with wire makes for an environment that encourages growth. Displaying them on a wall is fine if they get several hours of sun a day and air circulates well, but for air plants that particularly enjoy good ventilation, make sure to take them outside regularly.

Matching the Texture of a Tablecloth

Neither cut flowers nor potted plants, these individual table arrangements are sure to be the talk of any casual party. Lay down a faded linen cloth and group plenty of plants on to create volume. The slightly dry textural quality of air plants evokes a French or ethnic dining table.

● Materials and equipment

Air plants (eight of six different types)
Pumice stone
Glass containers

● Method

1

Pour pumice stone into containers, creating hollows in the surface of the stones to keep the large air plants stable.

2

Firstly, place the large plant that will form the focal point of the arrangement in the hollow. Lightly push unstable plants into the stones.

3

Create a richly expressive arrangement by choosing plants with strong leaf shapes that give the look of movement, plants of differing type, size and so on.

● Air plants used

A *Xerographica*
B *Vernicosa* purple giant
C *Ionantha* Ron
D *Ionantha variegate*
E *Stricta* hard leaf
F *Fasciculata*

● Display and care

Putting air plants together in one dish is a good way to make shifting them to sunny or breezy spots easy. Pumice stone absorbs water when plants are sprayed, allowing it to maintain a suitable level of moisture. Water to the extent that water does not collect in between the leaves of the *xerographica*. Even though this looks like a group planting, no soil is used so it makes for a neat and clean decoration for the dining table.

A Little Garden on Shelves

Here, potted plants line a wall-mounted shelf to form a little garden, transforming a wall into a charming space. The plants displayed are all types that, like air plants, prefer partial shade or the same amount of light as that filtered through a lace curtain, such as orchids and succulents. Potted plants with small flowers that change from day to day add to the enjoyment.

● Materials and equipment

Air plants
Driftwood
Wire
Radio pliers

● Method

1

Wind wire around the base of the air plant and twist it around driftwood to keep the plant in place.

2

Add the remaining air plants, considering the overall balance. Choose plants that differ in color, size and form to create dynamic effects.

● Display and care

Watering, care and so on are easiest when types that favor similar conditions in terms of direct sunlight, humidity levels and the like are brought together. Air does not circulate well at the back of deep shelves, so place shallow shelving somewhere with good ventilation. From time to time, place each pot outside in shade.

● Air plants used

A *Stricta* hard leaf
B *Capitata domingensis*
C *Latifolia* caulescent form
D *Tectorum*
E *Fasciculata*
F *Streptophylla*

Soft, Delicate Leaves Brighten a Dresser

A mirror, perfume and other objects line a dresser. You can see here how something as simple as placing air plants on top of the glass bottles softens the space in front of the mirror. The sophisticated silver tone of the leaves complements the jewelry-like string of little lights, while a feminine mood wafts from the soft leaves.

● Display and care
- These air plants are easily moved around, like ornaments, so can be easily rearranged, and it's easy to move them around as you tidy up your dresser.
- In spots that are some distance from windows, reflecting the light with a mirror is a way of ensuring brightness.
- Don't leave the plants in a room all the time, but ensure they get an airing by putting them outside every so often.

● Air plants used
Tectorum, *Stricta* hard leaf

Add Gentle Colors to a Work Space

When you want to open up your laptop or notebook, air plants are easily cleared away, like knick knacks. The green of their leaves soothes the eyes and increases working efficiency, making them a desirable item to have on a desk. Frosted glass windows let in just the right amount of light and make it easy to let in fresh air, so a spot like this is ideal for air plants.

● Display and care

· Place in a basket or net-like container for improved ventilation.
· It's good to have greenery in a space you use regularly. It reminds you to stop, look, and breathe. Having them in front of you makes it easy to remember to water them too.

● Air plants used

Tectorum, Ionantha, Stricta hard leaf, *Fasciculata hondurensis,* Twisted Tim, *Scaposa, Fuchsii fuchsii, Harrisii, Exserta*

Fixed to a Tree Branch Like Spring Buds

Little air plants bud on these branches, their subtle tones making them look exactly like new shoots. Why not try designing an arrangement using lots of different types on one branch, such as ones with green or with silver leaves, others with curly leaves and some that look like decorative balls? It's especially nice to see them together with real new growth in spring, after enjoying them attached to the bare branch.

● Materials and equipment

Air plants (13, of nine different types)
Tree branch
Wire
Radio pliers

● Method

1 Place the branch on a surface, the position the air plants along it, checking overall balance and keeping your desired finished result in mind.

2 Pass wire through the base of the air plants and wind it around the branch to secure plants, keeping in mind the direction the air plants will face.

The branch will be smooth and slippery so choose places where it forks or is easy to wind wire around.

● Air plants used

A *Fuchsii fuchsii*
B *Caput-medusae*
C *Velickiana*
D *Scaposa*
E *Tricolor*
F *Brachycaulos*
G *Capitata*
H *Tectorum*
I *Magnusiana*

● Display and care

Arranging small air plants on one branch gives them some presence. Additionally, attaching them to a branch makes it easier for them to grow, so it is effective when cultivating small plants. Use the forks of the branch or places where shoots are emerging as guides when attaching the air plants. Why not recycle by decorating a branch taken from garden prunings?

Displaying a Collection on an Old Display Rack

When your collection starts growing, it's fun displaying plants in a rack like this one. With its good ventilation, this item made of wire is perfect for an air plant display, and the shabby look of the iron brings out the subtle coloring of the air plants. Enjoy the overall look by not adding too many plants to the display.

● Display and care

· Display your air plants as you would a hobby collection.
· It is possible to display significant numbers of plants, but the trick is to use only enough plants to let the rack hold its own as a piece of decor.
· Once you have chosen the main plants, position the others to balance the composition.

● Air plants used

Brachycaulos, Scaposa, Tricolor *melanocrater, Exserta, Fuchsii fuchsii, Veluntina, Vernicosa* purple giant and so on

Mixed Together with Herbs in the Kitchen

Place them in empty jars or hang them—arrange them all over to create an upbeat mood in a kitchen that makes you want to cook. Air plants have well defined leaves, so match them with herbs with plentiful foliage to create a space that appears rich in greenery.

● Display and care

· A kitchen with a window is a bright place suitable for air plants.
· Humidity around the sink may seem to be of concern, but if the exhaust fan is switched on or the window is open this is actually a well ventilated spot.
· Plants' condition can be monitored and they can be watered as needed.

● Air plants used

Ionantha, Capitata, Stricta hard leaf, *Paleacea, Capitata domingensis, Tectorum*

A Simple Terrarium by the Window

Air plants enjoy in spreading out their leaves. This simple way of planting them makes for a stylish show. A terrarium made from a glass jar allows you to admire the plant from every aspect, which is sure to increase your affection for it. Here, the display is set next to a window which gets just the right shade from a garden tree.

● Materials and Air plants used

A *Butzii*
B *Harrisii*
C *Brachycaulos*
D *Caput-medusae*
E Tricolor

Use fine pumice stones with small plants. Prevent moldering by leaving space around the plants, making plantings that are just deep enough to keep the plants upright.

Use bark chips with large plants to create a natural look. The plant pictured is a Tricolor.

Green-leaved types cope relatively well with stuffy conditions, so are suited to terrariums.
The plant pictured is a *Bulbosa*.

Choose a long, thin container for plants with a long shape. This will serve to accentuate the line of jars.
The plant pictured is a Twisted Tim.

This silver-leaved type is particularly vulnerable to stuffy conditions, so choose a container with a wide opening for good ventilation.
The plant pictured is a *Fasciculata hondurensis*.

● Display and care

Green-leaved types which are intensely green in color are relatively resilient against moldering, so can be planted in a container with depth. For silver-leaved types, which are prone to moldering, choose a container with a wide aperture so that the air inside does not get stuffy. Do not close the containers. To water, spritz with water, place the container somewhere with good ventilation such as by a window. For types that can be cultivated without planting, make sure not to plant them too deeply in pumice stone. While the pumice stone absorbs excess water, a potted airplant can't be shaken to remove excess in the leaves, so don't go overboard when watering.

A Refreshingly Clean Accent

Arranged on a soap dish or hanging above the sink, the gentle green of air plants sets off the white walls and brings a refreshing sense of cleanliness. They can be displayed in the same way as other objects and work well around a cramped sink, but make sure they get good ventilation and occasionally place them outside.

● Display and care

· Displaying plants near the sink means you should be able to water regularly.
· Silver-leaved types can be cultivated relatively well in dark places, but require their air to be refreshed for more than half an hour each day.
· In particular, silver-leaved tectorums are a type that need drying out quickly after watering, so make sure they are well aired.

● Air plants used

Xerographica, Capitata, Tectorum, Usneoides

Old Containers by a Frosted Glass Window

Tin containers accent air plants displayed in front of a frosted glass window. The shabby tones of the tin match the pale green of the air plants and blend in with the wall color. A space with minimal color allows for savoring subtle differences in leaf color and texture, so choose carefully the varieties to display.

● Display and care
· The bark chips at the base of the tins retain just the right level of moisture to prevent drying out.
· A frosted glass window softens direct sunlight, letting in the kind of light air plants prefer.
· Make sure to put plants outside every so often.

● Air plants used
Capitata red, *Stricta* hard leaf

Delicate Colors Create a Bouquet for the Door

A beautiful plant with the slightest tinge of purple is the focal point for this wall decoration, which incorporates delicate silver and light green leaves and a red flower as an accent. Hang it from somewhere high so that you can enjoy the graceful stems as they trail down. Here, on a door with a large window, small, airy and light air plants like these are a good match.

● Materials and equipment

Air plants (six)
Wooden base (approx 4 in [10 cm])
Wire (two kinds: thick and fine)
Radio pliers

● Method

1

Firstly, wind fine wire around the base of the main air plant, then attach it to the wooden base.

2

Attach the other plants to the wooden base in the same way, finishing by winding thick wire around long-stemmed caulescent types to secure them to the base.

3

Form thick wire into a loop to hang the finished bouquet on the door.

4

The finished bouquet. Air plants grow slowly, so it won't lose its shape easily and can be enjoyed for a long time.

● Air plants used

A *Paleacea*
B *Andreana*
C *Tectorum*
D *Vernicosa* purple giant
E *Arhiza*
F *Arhiza-julieae x pruinosa*

● Display and care

Types with long stems create a natural flow, but break easily, so handle them carefully. A door under the eaves that is not in direct sun but receives a comfortable amount of light is a good spot to hang this arrangement. The plants favor the outdoors, so apart from winter when it drops below 32F/0C degrees or rains, it can be safely kept outside. If the backdrop is a grand, stately door, try using large types like Xerographica as the main plant.

A Touch of the Wild in an Old Birdcage

Don't you want to take a peek to see what's inside? Here, small air plants are displayed in old bird cages. Their soft, cotton-wool like texture and delicate figures are just like those of small birds. Their trailing growth has a wildness to it, making them seem to be on the point of escaping from their cages.

● Materials and equipment

Air plants (six)
Bird cages
Wire
Radio pliers

● Method

Attach cages to a wall. Use wire to secure air plants to give the look of plants trailing from the cage or sitting on perches like small birds.

● Air plants used

A *Paleacea*
B Tricolor
C *Mima chiletensis*
D *Arhiza-julieae x pruinosa*
E *Arhiza*
F *Stricta* hard leaf

● Display and care

This wall is semi-shaded and only gets a few hours of sunlight a day. As it is under the eaves, it is protected from rain and well ventilated, making it the perfect spot for air plants. On windy days, close the cage doors so plants will not be blown out. The stems of the caulescent plants are easily broken, so take care when removing dead leaves from the ends.

A Home for Plants in a Sun-Dappled Yard

An open bird feeder with a peaked roof is just like a home for air plants. In this garden comfortably lit by dappled sunlight, there's no need to worry about hot summer days or humidity and watering is easily done on the spot. The chic gray of the feeder works to accent the plant's green leaves.

● Materials and equipment

Air plants (five)
Bird feeders

● Method

These plants are simply placed in the bird feeders, but if they are secured with wire and placed on top of sphagnum moss, they will grow more quickly.

● Air plants used

A *Vernicosa* purple giant
B *Fasciculata*
C *Ionantha* Ron
D Twisted Tim
E *Harrisii*

● Display and care

Displaying plants in this way is the same as hanging them under the eaves of a house, so in snow-free regions they can be left outside all year round. However, cold winter rain can damage plants, so bring them inside during wet, cold weather. In cold, snowy regions, they must be brought indoors over winter. Use wire to secure plants to the feeders so that they won't fall out or be blown away by the wind.

Part 3

Air Plant Reference Guide

In this book, we introduce a total of 118 types of air plant—48 types that are easy to cultivate even for beginners, and 70 that appeal for their individuality. Refer to "How to use this guide" to find out more about various plants' characteristics and charms and to help you select varieties, care for and display plants.

How to use this guide

T. aeranthos ❶ ❷   ❸   ❹

Availability: average   Size: medium   Sunlight: B

❺ A caulescent variety with straight silver leaves that grow in rosette formation from an upright stem. Grows relatively quickly and flowers readily, making it a variety that is easy to cultivate even for beginners. Likes water, so use a spray bottle regularly and soak (see p20) during seasons when it dries out. Forms pups readily and clumps easily. Is resistant to cold, and in warm regions can be left outside all through winter. As its leaves are quite rigid, they break easily, so handle carefully.

❶ Variety/scientific name [T.] stands for Tillandsia family
❷ Relative ease of finding the plant
Easy: available at many stores including home centers
Average: readily available
Rare: only found in specialty stores
❸ Rough guide to size
Small: smaller than 4 in (10 cm) when in bloom
Medium: smaller than 8 in (20 cm) when in bloom
Large: all larger plants
❹ Rough guide to levels of sunlight (see diagram at right)
A: Place somewhere bright, like right next to a window
B: OK to be a slight distance from a window such as on a dining table
C: OK to be next to a wall or other spot with low light
❺ Characteristics
Basic appearance, distinguishing features, points to watch for when cultivating etc.

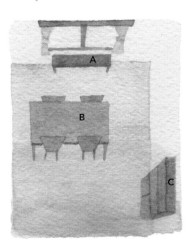

Easy-to-grow Varieties Recommended for Beginners

These varieties are relatively easy to come by and care for. Many of them are reasonably priced, so choose one that appeals to you and try cultivating it.

T. aeranthos

Availability: average   Size: medium   Sunlight: B

A caulescent variety with straight silver leaves that grow in rosette formation from an upright stem. Grows relatively quickly and flowers readily, making it a variety that is easy to cultivate even for beginners. Likes water, so use a spray bottle regularly and soak (see p20) during seasons when it dries out. Forms pups readily and clumps easily. Is resistant to cold, and in warm regions can be left outside all through winter. As its leaves are quite rigid, they break easily, so handle carefully.

T. araujei

Availability: average   Size: medium   Sunlight: A

A strongly built and vigorous grower. As it is a green-leaved variety and likes water, regular misting is effective. It comes in various strains and variations, all with attractive flowers, with one of its defining features being the long blooming period. It is caulescent and grows towards the sun, exaggeratedly twisting its stem as it does so.

T. andreana

Availability: average   Size: medium   Sunlight: A

An attractive green-leaved variety with fine leaves that open out in a spherical shape. It likes water, but dislikes water collecting between the leaves at its base and can start to rot if left soaking for a long period. The leaves break easily so water only by spraying. It is relatively vulnerable to the cold so in winter, keep it somewhere above 50F/10C degrees with little temperature variation.

T. ionantha

Availability: easy   Size: small   Sunlight: A

One of the most widely known air plant varieties and one of the easiest to come by, it originates from various places. It has many strains, all of which are suited to environments that are bright and have plenty of water and good ventilation. Some plants are silver in color but should be treated as green-leaved.

T. ionantha (Mexican form)

Availability: average

Size: small

Sunlight: A

This *ionantha* originates in Mexico. Like the *Fuego* (below), it turns red before blooming. It is characterized by its tendency to form clumps.

T. ionantha var.stricta forma fastigiata

Availability: average

Size: small

Sunlight: A

A hybrid variety of *ionantha* commonly known as "peanut." In comparison with other *ionantha* whose leaves form rosettes, its leaves do not spread out and instead grow in a straight configuration.

T. ionantha "Rubra"

Availability: average

Size: small

Sunlight: A

The plant pictured is in its normal condition, but particularly before blooming, it may change color to an attractive pale pastel pink. For an *ionantha*, it has relatively soft, fine and delicate leaves. This cultivar is from Guatemala.

T. ionantha "Fuego"

Availability: average

Size: small

Sunlight: A

Like the *Rubra*, the entire plant turns a vivid red as the blooming period draws closer. For an *ionantha*, it has particularly fine, dense foliage that makes for a delicate appearance.

T. ionantha (Guatemalan form)

Availability: easy

Size: small

Sunlight: A

A variety native to Guatemala, in the north of central America. Most air plants going by the name *ionantha* are this variety.

A type with delicate, curled leaves. The intricately tangled leaves are prone to moldering, so cultivate somewhere with good ventilation.

Leaves on the left are straight and large, while those on the right are fine and curled.

This type has large, straight leaves. Its hardiness makes it ideal for a beginner.

T. usneoides

Availability: easy   Size: large   Sunlight: B

Although this is a silver-leaved type, it is one of the most water-loving air plants. To maintain its attractive appearance, water and soak regularly. In its native habitat it winds itself around tree branches, telegraph wires and so on. It is a fast grower and its trailing foliage can reach a length that is more than the height of a person. Also known as Spanish moss, it is used ornamentally in *ikebana* and as a mulch, flower basket liner and more. The thickness and shape of the leaves can vary, but all *usneoides* have small yellow flowers.

T. caulescens

Availability: average

Size: medium

Sunlight: A

Caulescens comes from Latin and means "having a stem." As per its name, it has a long, undulating upright stem. It is characterized by its firm, pointed leaves like that of a pine tree. It is a green-leaved variety and likes mid-air environments with high levels of humidity, so regular misting is necessary. The leaves are straight and rigid.

T. cacticola

Availability: average

Size: large

Sunlight: A

In its native habitat, this plant attaches itself to cacti, and it is said that its name is derived from this. It is extremely hardy and resilient against dryness, and grows to a large size. There are many different forms available, making it fun to build a collection even within the one variety. It may appear slightly silver, but is a green-leaved type with foliage that is on the soft side.

T. gardneri

Availability: average

Size: medium

Sunlight: A

Covered in extremely attractive trichomes (p10), this is a typical silver-leaved variety. If attached to a cork board or tree fern slab and hung in mid-air somewhere where it can catch the breeze, its attractive form is easily maintained. It is extremely delicate and if it dries out, it is prone to wrinkling and discoloration at the tips of the leaves which is difficult to remedy, so make sure to water regularly. Take particular care in summer when it has a tendency to molder.

T. capitata

Availability: easy

Size: large

Sunlight: A

This green-leaved variety has bright, glossy leaves. It is one of the varieties which likes moisture and will thrive if given plenty of water. The leaves are thin so watch out for leaf burn due to strong sunlight. It is possible to cultivate this variety by planting it in a pot with pumice stone, bark chips and the like. It comes in various strains and hybrids.

T. capitata "Red"

Availability: average

Size: large

Sunlight: A

A red-leaved variety of *capitata*. Like the *capitata*, its leaves burn easily if it gets strong sun, but if it doesn't get enough sunlight the leaves will turn green. The leaves of this plant are plentiful and rigid and it likes a lot of water. If the light conditions are favorable the whole plant from the new bud in the center to the outer leaves will take on an attractive color.

T. caput-medusae

Availability: average

Size: medium

Sunlight: A

This popular variety has a swollen, pot-shaped form with a scientific name meaning "head of Medusa." It forms clumps easily and is a hardy, vigorous grower. The leaves grow in irregular directions, twisting and undulating as they grow. It likes sunlight, so should be cultivated somewhere undercover outdoors such as under the eaves from spring to fall, but make sure to keep it out of strong sun in summer. Although it has a whitish appearance, it is a green-leaved variety.

T. xerographica

Availability: average

Size: large

Sunlight: A

This plant is usually classified as a tank type, but as it is relatively resilient to dryness it is usual to cultivate it without potting it. It is a silver-leaved type but likes sun, so cultivate it beside a window where it is bright. As it is comparatively vulnerable to cold and its growing point (core) can rot easily, avoid putting it anywhere that gets too cold overnight or in the morning. A giant variety with considerable presence, it makes a perfect focal point. The plant in the photo is about five years old. Parent plants last about a year after flowering.

Geminiflora means "twin flower." It has two flowers that bud from the one flower bract.

T. geminiflora

Availability: average

Size: medium

Sunlight: A

While it resembles a *stricta* (p65), this plant has comparatively softer leaves that spread out, radiating from the center. It is a sturdy, easily grown green-leaved variety that likes water so can be cultivated in a pot. The attractive pink and purple flowers are extremely gorgeous and it is a variety which flowers readily, but at only one week, its blooming season is shorter than regular air plants.

T. crocata

Availability: average

Size: medium

Sunlight: A

This silver-leaved variety is characterized by its fine, undulating leaves covered in trichomes. While its color and texture are similar to that of *usneoides* (p57), it grows in a spherical shape. It likes places with high levels of humidity and ample sunlight. As it clumps easily, it doesn't like being left damp for long periods of time, so place it somewhere in the path of a breeze to prevent moldering. The scented flowers are small and yellow. It grows well when attached to something like a cork board.

T. concolor

Availability: average

Size: medium

Sunlight: A

A vigorously growing popular variety, it has quite firm, long green leaves that radiate from the center, creating an attractive appearance. The leaves break easily, so when soaking, use a large bucket and make sure not to force the plant into the water. Similarly, make sure it has space when putting it on display. Spraying on liquid fertilizer during the growth period is effective for achieving faster growth.

T. jucunda

Availability: average

Size: medium

Sunlight: A

An attractive silver-leaved variety with bluish-white leaves that grow in neat rosette form, creating a beautiful appearance. The leaves have a hard texture and taper to a fine point at the ends. As they break easily, take care when soaking, handling and so on as per the *concolor* above. As flowering season nears, the center of the plant changes color to turn a shade of pale pink.

T. juncifolia

Availability: easy

Size: medium

Sunlight: A

Of the grass types, this is a variety with predominantly green leaves, with some individual plants having a red tinge. Although extremely similar to a *juncea* (below), this plant takes slightly longer to grow and likes plenty of water. Water collects easily in the base and may cause rot to set in, so make sure to get rid of excess water by turning the plant upside down after watering.

T. juncea

Availability: easy

Size: medium

Sunlight: A

This typical grass type has straight, dense leaves that do not spread out but grow straight up. A silver-leaved variety, it has minute trichomes. It is hardy and relatively resilient against dryness, growing vigorously. It forms pups readily and clumps easily. It twists and bends as it grows towards the light.

T. scaposa

Availability: easy
Size: medium
Sunlight: B

This plant resembles the *ionantha* (p56) but is characterized by its leaves, which all bend in the same direction. Its country of origin is relatively cool and mountainous so it is resilient against cold and can tolerate temperatures as low as about 41F/5C degrees, but does not cope well with the high temperatures and humidity of summer. A silver-leaved variety, it is prone to moldering, so ventilation is of utmost priority. If attached to a tree fern slab or something similar its growth will improve and care will be relatively easy.

T. streptophylla

Availability: average
Size: medium
Sunlight: A

One of the popular silver-leaved varieties. It is characterized by the way its form resembles a dwarf version of a xerographica (p62) but the leaves in the upper section are slightly upright. The leaves are soft and curl tightly into balls when they do not have enough water. Due to its form, water collects easily between the leaves and the plant is prone to rot, so after watering, make sure the plant is well aired and any moisture on the surface can dry out.

T. stricta

Availability: average
Size: large
Sunlight: B

This variety is a particularly good bloomer. It is defined by its hardiness, ready growth and tendency to clump and likes sun and water. It sprouts many new leaves which grow densely, so prevent moldering by regularly removing withred or old foliage and maintaining good ventilation. Apart from the soft leaves of the basic variety, there are several other types including a hard leaf variety. This is a green-leaved variety.

T. stricta hybrid

Availability: rare
Size: large
Sunlight: B

Stricta have been crossed with different varieties to create beautiful hybrids. Depending on the parent plant, some remarkable variations occur in leaf and flower appearance. The unique results make these plants interesting to collect. While many of the hybrids are extremely rare, they tend to share the hardiness of their *stricta* parent.

T. seleriana

Availability: easy
Size: large
Sunlight: C

This air plant is typical of the pot types. A silver-leaved variety, it has leaves covered in many trichomes and is soft and fluffy to the touch. Its form allows water to collect easily at the base, so after watering the plant must be turned upside down to shake off excess water and should be placed somewhere that air circulates well. It cannot tolerate direct sunlight so can be cultivated even in a spot that gets little sun. When purchasing, hold the plant in your hand to select stock that has some weight to it.

T. seleriana "Special"

Availability: rare
Size: large
Sunlight: C

Of the *selerianas*, the leaf formation and volume of output set this plant apart and it is known as "special." It is worth keeping in mind that its availability is patchy, with many on the market at some times, followed by complete lack of availability at others. Points to keep in mind when cultivating are the same as for the *seleriana*.

T. tectorum

Availability: average
Size: large
Sunlight: A

A popular silver-leaved variety. In its country of origin, this plant grows naturally on cliffs in high altitudes of about 6500-6600 feet (2000 m) where there is little mist, so has developed trichomes to take in moisture. To maintain its attractive appearance, make sure it gets the right amount of light and ventilation, and after watering, place somewhere that will allow moisture to dry out quickly. Too much water will cause the number of trichomes to decrease so don't be too heavy handed. There are many different forms of this plant in circulation.

T. harrisii
Availability: easy
Size: medium
Sunlight: A

An entry-level silver-leaved variety, this plant is characterized by its rosette shape and leaves that curl in helix-like formation. The leaves are soft and easily snapped or scratched, so to maintain its attractive appearance, thought must be given to where the plant is kept. Water collects readily in the base of the plant, so after watering, turn it upside down to shake off excess water.

T. fasciculata
Availability: average
Size: large
Sunlight: A

A popular variety, this plant grows considerably large and has an attractive appearance. Its silver leaves radiate from the center, boldly spreading out. This plant is relatively fond of water and requires regular misting and, in some cases, soaking. It puts out roots readily so can be grown in a pot. It is a silver-leaved variety.

T. filifolia

Availability: average

Size: medium

Sunlight: A

A popular green-leaved variety characterized by its long, fine, soft filament-like leaves. The base of the plant is brown, while the new shoots are a vibrant green color. Its appeal lies in its unique delicacy, so display it to set off its individuality. As it is relatively vulnerable to dryness, the secret to maintaining its attractive appearance is regular misting. It is light, so make sure it is not blown away if kept outdoors on windy days. If displayed with a type of a different appearance, the individualities of each plant will be set off effectively.

T.fuchsii var. fuchsii

Availability: average

Size: medium

Sunlight: A

A basic variety of the *fuchsii*, this plant has fleshier leaves and is firmer than the *gracilis* (p69). It is extremely popular thanks to its attractive appearance with the whitish silver leaves growing densely like a burr. When purchasing, choose a plant whose leaf tips are intact and that feels like it has some weight when you hold it in your hand.

T. fuchsii gracilis

Availability: average

Size: medium

Sunlight: A

The extremely delicate leaves of this plant charm, but snap easily, so when soaking, soak the plant by itself. If the air is dry, the pretty silver leaves go brown and start withering from the tips, but regular misting will prevent this. When the plant blooms, it shoots out a long, thin flower stem that resembles a sparkler.

T. butzii

Availability: easy

Size: medium

Sunlight: B

This popular variety stands out for the stripes around its pot-like base. Its leaves grow in long waves like unruly hair, with those in the photo approximately 16 in (40 cm) long with a texture similar to leather cord. A sturdy, fast-growing green-leaved variety, even if it doesn't flower it will form pups and readily clump. It is easy to come by. It is relatively fond of water so rather than only misting, should be soaked as well.

T. tenuifolia

Availability: average

Size: medium

Sunlight: B

This plant has quite firm, fine leaves and small pale blue flowers. It closely resembles the *stricta* (p65) but it seems common for this plant to have fewer leaves. Depending on the environment in which it is cultivated, its form can change dramatically. It is a green-leaved variety, but can be cultivated even in places with quite poor sunlight.

T. duratii

Availability: average

Size: large

Sunlight: C

A caulescent type characterized by thick, tough leaves that trail down and curl at the ends, creating a unique appearance. It can get extremely large. If placed on a table or other surface, its leaves can break or get crushed, so to continue enjoying its attractive appearance, hang it from somewhere like the ceiling. A silver-leaved variety, it is relatively tolerant to dryness and darkness.

T. tricolor

Availability: average

Size: medium

Sunlight: C

A hardy, green-leaved type with rigid leaves that make an impression thanks to their gradation of color. In bloom, the red and yellow of the flower head and the purple of the flower are all on show, with these three colors (tricolor) lending the plant its name. The main variety is similar to a tank type in some regards, and like a *punctulata*, is structured in a way that water collects around the base and is possible to cultivate in a pot. However, it has a tendency to molder in an enclosed room, so cultivate it somewhere with decent ventilation.

T.paucifolia

Availability: average

Size: large

Sunlight: B

A variety with rather fleshy leaves that copes well with heat. If raised under cover outdoors from spring to summer and given plenty of water, it will thrive, becoming plump and filling out. As it is a silver-leaved type, it can grow even in a spot where light is poor. It does not cope well with the cold in winter so over this season should be kept somewhere warmer than 50F/10C degrees.

T. brachycaulos

Availability: easy

Size: medium

Sunlight: A

A typical green-leaved variety with several strains, it likes water and humidity, so daily misting is key to keeping it looking good. For this reason, though, this plant is prone to moldering, so make sure it is kept well aired. It is a fast grower and puts out roots readily, so can be cultivated attached to driftwood and so on. If light conditions are favorable, it may acquire a reddish tinge.

T. puruinosa

Availability: average

Size: medium

Sunlight: A

A popular variety that is small and pot-shaped, this silver-leaved variety is defined by its undulating leaves and subtle shades which form an attractive gradation. The leaf surfaces are covered in trichomes and the plant feels light and fluffy when placed in the hand. It likes water, but water tends to collect in the gaps between leaves, so make sure to hold upside down after watering to shake off excess and give it a good airing. Prior to flowering, the entire plant turns a deep reddish purple shade.

T. bulbosa

Availability: easy

Size: medium

Sunlight: B

A popular pot-shaped variety characterized by its soft cylindrical leaves that grow in undulations from the base. It is a relatively fast grower, sprouting roots straight away if placed in a humid, bright spot. As leaves burn in direct sunlight, a spot that gets soft light like that filtered through lace curtains is ideal. Water tends to collect at the plant base, so turn the plant upside down to shake off excess water after watering. Treat as a green-leaved variety, making sure it doesn't dry out too much.

T. funckiana

Availability: average

Size: medium

Sunlight: A

This caulescent variety has fine leaves that form a shape like a squirrel's tail. It is a green-leaved variety that turns red when kept in a bright spot. It likes water, but tends to molder and shrivel up when kept in an enclosed space, so place somewhere well ventilated, particularly after watering. Regular misting is effective. A comparatively fast grower, it forms clumps readily. It is a member of the *andreana* family (p55) and does not cope with cold, so keep it somewhere above 50F/10C degrees in winter.

T. punctulata

Availability: average

Size: large

Sunlight: A

A tank type, this plant can be cultivated in a pot or as is. As it is a green-leaved variety with grass-like leaves and is relatively fond of water, make sure it is well aired and does not molder. If it suddenly receives strong light the leaves will curl up, so when placing outside do it gradually and make sure it doesn't receive direct western sunlight. If cultivated in a pot it may grow to more than 12 in (30 cm) tall.

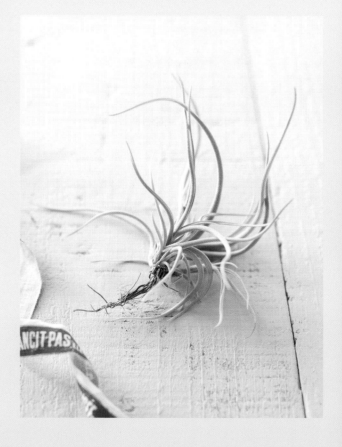

T. baileyi

Availability: average

Size: medium

Sunlight: B

A hardy pot-type variety with comparatively fleshy, thick, long leaves that grow in helix formation. The leaves are soft and silver. It is a relatively fast grower and puts out roots readily, making it easy to attach to a cork board, driftwood and so on. Even if it does not flower, it produces pups readily and forms clumps as in the photo.

T. velickiana

Availability: average

Size: medium

Sunlight: A

A silver-leaved variety, this plant creates a graceful impression with its long, soft, white leaves that radiate out from its center. It loves water, so make sure to mist every day. A lack of water quickly causes the leaves to curl inwards. The leaves snap or damage easily so if soaking or carrying out other tasks, make sure to handle the plant individually. It is a relatively fast grower.

T. reichenbachii

Availability: average

Size: medium

Sunlight: A

Forms vary in individual plants of this variety, which has rigid leaves which grow in uneven waves. It is a silver-leaved variety that closely resembles a dwarf version of the *duratii* (p70). Its leaves snap easily, so handle with care. It likes water but if ventilation is poor its lower leaves turn black, so if keeping indoors, make sure to thoroughly refresh air regularly. The flowers have a jasmine-like scent.

Specialty Varieties

With unique foliage formations, flowers and other features, these 70 varieties are overflowing with charm. Included among them are rare plants which can be found at specialty stores and varieties that are difficult to cultivate.

*See p54 for how to use this reference guide.

T. aff. duratii

Availability: rare   Size: medium   Sunlight: A

A species related to *duratii* (p70) requiring similar methods of cultivation. aff means affinis and means "to resemble." The downward-hanging leaves are similar, but it is slightly smaller and the leaves differ in thickness. It grows faster than the duratii and likes sunlight. Hang it up to display its attractive form most effectively. It is a silver-leaved variety.

T. aff. boliviensis "Blue Flower"

Availability: rare   Size: medium   Sunlight: A

Related to *boliviensis*, this species has fleshy, firm leaves that radiate from the center. Its silver leaves are covered in short trichomes. Although easy to cultivate, it grows best when attached to a support such as a tree fern slab. Flowering differs between individual plants, but contrary to the plant's name, many have pale pink blooms.

T. aeranthos "Purple Giant"

Availability: rare   Size: large   Sunlight: A

A relatively fast grower, this is a variety of the *aeranthos* (p55), a plant that is easy even for beginners to cultivate, and grows to a giant size as its name suggests. It is a silver-leaved plant that takes on reddish purple tones. Keep it in natural light to enjoy its attractive colorations.

T. aeranthos "Mini Purple"
Availability: rare   Size: medium   Sunlight: A

An extremely hardy variety of the *aeranthos*, this is a dwarf variety that takes on quite a reddish purple color. It has rigid silver leaves. Resilient to dryness and cold, in temperate regions it may be cultivated outside year round.

T. atroviridipetala "Large Form"
Availability: rare Size: medium   Sunlight: A

Although it resembles the *pulmosa* (p89), the leaves of this plant are more rigid and it is a silver-leaved variety covered all over in short trichomes. In hot, muggy and overly humid conditions it is prone to rot, so take particular care over summer.

T. arhiza-juliae x pruinosa
Availability: rare   Size: medium   Sunlight: A

This is a silver-leaved hybrid that has the characteristics of the two popular pot-type varieties from which it is created, that is, it is swollen at the base. It is relatively easy to cultivate, but in the summer months, it can be damaged if water is left to collect in its base, so after watering make sure to shake off any excess droplets.

T. albida
Availability: rare Size: large   Sunlight: A

This silver-leaved caulescent variety is covered in fine snow-white trichomes, making it very attractive. However, the leaves are quite rigid and are easily damaged or snapped. Maintain its beautiful appearance by hanging it or allowing it to take root on a board or other structure. It is a slow grower but extremely robust.

T. albertiana

Availability: rare   **Size:** small   **Sunlight:** A

A green-leaved variety with fleshy, deep green leaves. If cultivated under good light conditions the entire plant will turn a silver gray with subtle shadings. It is a relatively fast grower and is a robust plant. It is easier to cultivate if attached to a board or other structure. Its crimson flowers are particularly attractive.

T. ionantha var. van-hyningii

Availability: rare   **Size:** medium   **Sunlight:** A

A variety of *ionantha* (p56), this hybrid grows from a stem and stands upright. It is slower to grow than other *ionantha*. While it is a green-leaved variety, the entire plant turns red prior to flowering. It does not tolerate cold well, so take care when watering over winter and place in a spot where the temperature remains constant.

T. ionantha "Fat Boy"

Availability: average **Size:** medium **Sunlight:** A

There are relatively large volumes circulating of this plant. Among the *ionanthas*, the plant that typifies air plants, it is one of the larger varieties. A vigorous grower, it also flowers and, as it produces pups readily, it clumps easily.

T. ionantha "Druido"

Availability: rare   **Size:** medium   **Sunlight:** A

While purple flowers are usual among the *ionantha*, this variety has white flowers. In favorable conditions with plenty of constant sunshine, it is distinguished by the way its leaves turning yellow prior to flowering. Allowing it to take root to a tree fern slab or other structure ensures its health.

T. ionantha "Mardi Grass"
Availability: rare   Size: medium   Sunlight: A

In favorable conditions with good sunlight the tips of the leaves of this green-leaved variety turn scarlet. Compared with other *ionantha*, the leaves are quite fine and delicate. They are covered with many trichomes which appear white when the plant dries out. Cultivate in the same way as other *ionantha*.

T. ionantha var. "Maxima"
Availability: rare   Size: large   Sunlight: A

This green-leaved variety is a giant among *ionantha*. Its short, stout, compact growing leaves give the plant a heavy feel in the hand. It is relatively easy to cultivate and grows fast, but as the leaves grow densely, it is susceptible to moldering and needs to be kept somewhere with good ventilation. The leaves burn easily if they receive strong sunlight.

T. ionantha "Ron"
Availability: rare   Size: small   Sunlight: A

This plant is small even for an *ionantha*. Its rather fleshy, short leaves curl slightly outwards, giving it a cute appearance. In conditions with good sunlight, its central section takes on a yellow tone prior to flowering. Enjoy the attractive gradations in color of this green-leaved variety.

T. ixioides
Availability: rare   Size: medium   Sunlight: A

A silver-leaved type, its rigid leaves curl subtly inwards to form a neat rosette shape. It grows most reliably if attached to something such as a tree fern slab. If water is allowed to collect in its center the plant will start to rot from the base of its leaves, so after watering turn upside down to shake off excess droplets.

T. ixioides "Dwarf"
Availability: rare   Size: small   Sunlight: A

This is a dwarf variety of *ixioides* (p79). Like *ixioides*, it has rigid silver leaves and grows in an attractive star formation. Although it is a slow grower, it is relatively hardy, forms pups readily and clumps easily. It is unusual among air plants as it has yellow flowers, which have a faint perfume.

T. ixioides x T. duratii
Availability: rare   Size: large   Sunlight: A

A hybrid of *ixioides* (p79) and *duratii* (p70). In form it has taken on the characteristics of the duratii and grows upright as if it had a spine. It is a hardy silver-leaved variety that is easy to cultivate. The flowers are blue and extremely beautiful, with pups forming readily after blooming.

T. vernicosa "Giant Form"
Availability: rare   Size: large   Sunlight: A

A variety of *vernicosa* with fleshy, rigid leaves that spread out into a rosette. Its relatively long, softly curling leaves create an elegant appearance that makes an impression. The long, rigid leaves break and damage easily, so handle with care. It is an attractive silver-leaved variety that grows to a considerable size.

T. vernicosa "Purple Giant"
Availability: rare   Size: large   Sunlight: A

Of all the giant varieties that grow in rosette formation, this silver-leaved variety is a particularly handsome example. In poor sunlight, the entire plant acquires a green tone, but in good conditions the copper leaves turn a faintly red-purple shade that is extremely pretty. In overly strong sun, the leaves will burn, so it is to be avoided, especially in summer when extra care should be taken.

T. extensa "Red Form"

Availability: rare   Size: large   Sunlight: A

Extensa is a vigorously growing giant variety with long, elegantly spreading leaves. The plant turns red from the center, and in conditions with good sunlight the entire plant turns an attractive red color. It is covered in short trichomes, but requires plenty of water and may be cultivated in a pot. A silver-leaved variety, it is hardy and forms pups readily.

T. exserta

Availability: rare   Size: large   Sunlight: B

A silver-leaved giant variety. It is relatively resistant to cold and can be kept outdoors undercover in winter as long as the minimum temperature is more than 41F/5C degrees. Its long leaves are rigid and curl elegantly, and its beauty is best maintained by hanging the plant to care for it. The leaves snap easily, so handle with care.

T. cauligera

Availability: rare   Size: large   Sunlight: A

A robust, caulescent silver-leaved variety with rigid leaves. Covered with trichomes that make it appear white, it tolerates dryness relatively well but an extreme lack of water will make the leaves curl in vertically, just as for other varieties. It is lightweight, so if keeping it outside make sure that it is not blown away and that the leaves do not snap.

T. capitata "Domingensis"

Availability: rare   Size: medium   Sunlight: A

An attractive plant that is completely wine red in color. Among the green-leaved varieties of *capitata* (p59) it has a relatively high number of trichomes and the leaves are slightly rigid. It does not cope well with cold and should be kept in a spot where the minimum temperature is more than 50F/10C degrees. It puts out roots readily, so is recommended for beginners who would like to display it attached to an object on a wall.

T. capillaris
Availability: rare   Size: small   Sunlight: A

While it is a dwarf silver-leaved variety, this plant is easily divided and clumps readily. Many individual plants growing in colonies thrive, but they are prone to moldering and should be hung somewhere with good ventilation for proper care. Ideally, cultivate it in a bright spot near a window where the temperature is constant, as this plant does not like extreme changes in temperature.

T. xiphioides "Fuzzy Form"
Availability: rare   Size: medium   Sunlight: A

This plant has fleshy, slightly rigid silver leaves that curl at the tips like the crest of a wave. It is covered all over in long, thick trichomes that make it appear an attractive silver gray in natural light. It has white, scented flowers. From the formation of buds until flowers blossom is a lengthy process that can take several months.

T. geminif lora x T. recurvifolia
Availability: rare   Size: medium   Sunlight: A

A hybrid, this green-leaved variety has relatively soft leaves which radiate out from the center. It is hardy and if kept under cover, can be cultivated outdoors all year round. Like its parent varieties, it likes water, so mist it regularly to maintain its attractive appearance. In minimum temperatures of more than 59F/15C degrees it is fine to shower it directly with water too.

T. comarapaensis
Availability: rare   Size: medium   Sunlight: A

Similarly to *ixioides* (p80), this plant has rigid silver leaves that form a rosette. Its name is derived from Comarapa, the place in its native land, Bolivia, where it was discovered. In extreme dryness the tips of its leaves turn brown, so make sure to mist regularly. Its leaves snap easily so care for it by attaching it to something and hanging it up.

T. concolor x T. ionantha
Availability: rare   Size: medium   Sunlight: A

A hybrid of the two varieties which make up its name, this green-leaved variety has long leaves that resemble stretched-out tape versions of *ionantha* leaves (p56). It is hardy but vulnerable to cold, so keep it in a bright spot that is more than 50F/10C degrees. It responds well to liquid fertilizer so if the minimum temperature is more than 59F/15C degrees, apply it once a month to achieve good growth.

T. concolor x T. streptophylla
Availability: rare   Size: medium   Sunlight: A

This plant is a hybrid variety of the hardy *concolor* (p62) and the popular pot-type *streptophylla* (p64). Like its parent varieties, it is fond of water so if it dries out, soak it and then make sure to shake off excess water. It does not cope well with cold, so keep it in a spot where air circulates well and the temperature remains constant. It is a green-leaved variety.

T. schatzlii
Availability: rare   Size: medium   Sunlight: A

Short trichomes cover the rigid, fleshy silver leaves of this plant, giving it the look of glossy shark skin. It has few leaves, some of which curl and some of which grow straight, making for differences between individual plants. Its new growth is somewhat irregular, but it develops roots relatively readily and if allowed to attach to something its growth will stabilize. Its base is prone to rotting, so make sure it is kept well aired.

T. jonesi
Availability: rare   Size: medium   Sunlight: A

If touched with a fingertip, the rigid leaves of this plant can inflict pain. Like a caulescent plant, this silver-leaved variety grows by extending its central growing point. If not in the direct path of a cold wind, it can tolerate temperatures as low as 32F/0C degrees. It turns green in environments where the light is dim, so to maintain the attractive purple-red shade, keep it out of direct rays but ensure it gets plenty of sunlight.

T. sucrei
Availability: rare   Size: small   Sunlight: A

A dwarf variety, this plant has beautiful silver leaves covered with long, fluffy trichomes. Its soft, delicate leaves are easily deformed, so handle carefully, preferably attaching the plant to something such as a tree fern slab. From spring to summer during the plant's growth period, it should be kept somewhere with good ventilation such as under the eaves. It has large peach-colored flowers.

T. stellifera
Availability: rare   Size: medium   Sunlight: A

This silver-leaved variety is covered all over with feathery trichomes that turn it a beautiful pure white. It is robust and can withstand minimum temperatures as low as about 41F/5C degrees, but it is a remarkably slow grower. Once damaged, it is difficult to restore its attractive appearance, so it is crucial to keep it out of strong natural light and ensure that it is well aired. It is best to keep it hung up.

T. stricta piniformis
Availability: rare   Size: medium   Sunlight: A

The leaves of this plant grow in a spiral fashion, creating a long teardrop shaped form. A silver-leaved variety, its rigid silver-gray leaves are glossy and attractive. As is the case for the basic variety, this variety is easy to cultivate. In its growth period from spring to summer its attractive appearance can be maintained through giving it plenty of water, such as by showering it with water as well as misting.

T. stricta "Pink Bronze"
Availability: rare   Size: medium   Sunlight: A

As per the basic variety, this green-leaved plant is robust and easy to cultivate even for beginners. If it receives plenty of sun the tips of its leaves turn bronze, deepening in color if the plant is allowed to take root. It flowers readily, with the flower bract a pale pink that blossoms with a pretty blue flower. It is resilient against heat but must be kept well aired.

T. secunda var. "Major"
Availability: rare   Size: large   Sunlight: A

A hybrid variety of the secunda, this plant is characterized by its silver leaves which form a rosette. Similarly to a green leaved plant, it likes water and good ventilation and in its growth period from spring to summer should be showered with water in the evening. After watering, turn the plant upside down to get rid of excess water. It is possible to cultivate in a pot. It is resilient against heat but dislikes cold.

T. chiapensis
Availability: rare   Size: medium   Sunlight: A

This silver-leaved variety has rigid, fleshy, twisting leaves that are covered all over with trichomes that resemble short hairs. It looks white, but has red pigment cells that are stimulated by plentiful sunlight, causing the plant to change color. It grows relatively slowly, putting forth a large flower head that extends over several months before flowering. It forms pups readily.

T. diaguitensis
Availability: rare   Size: medium   Sunlight: A

Although closely resembling the *paleacea* (p87), the leaves of this silver-leaved variety are finer and it readily forms large clumps. The leaves are rigid and are susceptible to snapping and damage, so it is a good idea to attach it to something such as driftwood and hang it upside down. The attractive branches radiate out from the center. Regular watering is necessary. The plant has extremely beautiful white flowers.

T. didisticha
Availability: rare   Size: large   Sunlight: A

This attractive silver-leaved variety has fleshy leaves which undulate and twist as they radiate out. It has many leaves and is prone to moldering, so keep it somewhere well ventilated. It is a slow grower that requires some time to achieve significant growth. If the minimum temperature is around 41F/5C degrees, it is possible to cultivate it outside under eaves or somewhere similar.

T. tenuifolia vaginata

Availability: rare   Size: large   Sunlight: A

A variety of *tenuifolia* (p70), this unique green-leaved variety grows in a form resembling a squirrel's tail. The leaves are rigid with pointy tips. It is a hardy variety that is easy to cultivate and grows relatively quickly, clumping readily as in the photograph. It likes plenty of water, so make sure to water its leaves regularly from spring to summer.

T. nidus (T. ionantha x T. fasciculata)

Availability: rare   Size: large   Sunlight: A

A hybrid of two varieties, the base of this plant with its dense foliage resembles the *ionantha* (p56), while the tips of the leaves radiate out like the *fasciculata* (p67). At minimum temperatures of more than 50F/10C degrees it may be kept outdoors, and should be watered regularly, using the showering method and so on. A green-leaved variety, it should be kept out of direct sun but turns an attractive red when it receives appropriate amounts of light.

T. neglecta

Availability: rare   Size: medium   Sunlight: A

A caulescent green-leaved variety with slightly rigid, dense foliage. It is robust and easy to cultivate, growing relatively quickly. It forms pups readily and clumps easily. Hang it outside under the eaves or somewhere similar from spring to summer, taking care that the leaves do not burn. It has extremely beautiful purple flowers.

T. neglecta "Small Form"

Availability: rare   Size: small   Sunlight: A

This green-leaved variety has short leaves and a compact appearance over all. It is prone to moldering, and after watering, ideally should be placed in a well-ventilated spot or, if indoors, somewhere where the air can be refreshed regularly. Placing it on top of bark chips for planting western orchids allows for moisture regulation and encourages root development.

T. neglecta "Rubra"
Availability: rare   Size: small   Sunlight: A

An attractively colored green-leaved variety closely related to *neglecta*. Its coloration depends on the environment in which it is grown, so to enjoy a deep, vibrant color, make sure it gets plenty of sun during its growth period. It has a tendency to be a little vulnerable to cold, but it is easy to care for and readily forms pups.

T. novakii
Availability: rare   Size: large   Sunlight: A

A silver-leaved variety that grows relatively quickly and is easy to cultivate. In a growth environment where it receives enough sun and air, the entire plant may turn a pretty pink shade, depending on the season. This is a plant that requires natural light. As it has long, rigid leaves, be careful not to snap them off when soaking or carrying out other tasks for its care.

T. bartrami
Availability: rare   Size: medium   Sunlight: A

In contrast to the impression it makes with its delicate, grass-like silver leaves, this plant has a high tolerance for both dryness and cold. There are not many of these plants on the market, but they are easy to cultivate. The plant may be potted and grows well in soil made from a mix of bark for western orchids, pumice stone and so on. It can be placed on sphagnum moss, but the moss holds water too well, so the arrangement must be kept in a well-ventilated spot.

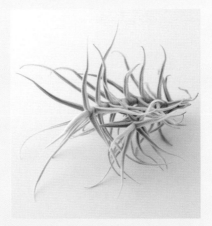

T. paleacea
Availability: rare   Size: large   Sunlight: A

A caulescent type with attractive silver leaves that appear white, this plant is shown as a clump in the photograph. It should be kept slightly dry, but during its growth period from spring to summer, responds well to its leaves being watered after sundown. During the day, any water droplets on the leaves act as a lens and may cause the leaves to burn. As it is a slightly heavy plant, if hanging, make sure it is well secured.

T. bandensis
Availability: rare   Size: medium   Sunlight: A

A green-leaved variety with a short stem and leaves that fan out, this plant likes water and does well in hot, humid conditions, but is particularly susceptible to moldering so proper ventilation is of top importance. If it is attached to something it clumps readily, as in the photograph. If keeping it outside, make sure it won't be blown away in the wind. This plant readily forms flower buds and blossoms with small, scented flowers.

T. fasciculata x T. xerographica
Availability: rare   Size: large   Sunlight: A

This hybrid variety has leaves that are straight like the fasciculata (p67) and wide like the xerographica (p60). An attractive giant silver-leaved variety, it is easily damaged so should be kept secured and soaking should be avoided. Make sure it is kept well aired and reduce the frequency of watering during cold periods.

T. fasciculata x T. hondurensis
Availability: rare   Size: medium   Sunlight: A

A natural hybrid, the characteristics of the *hondurensis* parent plant are slightly stronger, resulting in fleshy silver leaves with a bluish white tone. It is a vigorous grower but extremely prone to moldering, so is suited to being grown on driftwood, tree fern slabs and so on suspended in the air. Place in a well-ventilated place particularly in the summer months.

T. plagiotropica
Availability: rare   Size: small   Sunlight: A

An attractive dwarf variety that is relatively easy to come by, with slightly pale, soft green leaves radiating from its center. If placed in direct contact with a surface, the leaves are easily crushed, so attach it to driftwood or something similar. When soaking, make sure it does not become submerged under another plant. It likes water but is particularly prone to moldering.

T. bulbosa "Belize"
Availability: rare   Size: medium   Sunlight: A

A variety of *bulbosa* (p73), this green-leaved variety has just started to circulate in recent years. It is a hardy plant, and if given plenty of water and light and aired properly during its growth period from spring to summer, it will produce many new shoots. Watch out for leaf burn caused by direct sunlight in summer. When purchasing, look for a plant that feels heavy when you hold it.

T. pulmosa
Availability: average   Size: small   Sunlight: A

Pulmosa means "feathery." This attractive silver-leaved variety has delicate leaves densely covered with trichomes. If it molders, the entire plant turns black and its appearance is ruined, so proper ventilation is a must. It is particularly susceptible to damage in summer, and should be watered from the evening onwards when the temperature cools. The fine leaves snap easily so handle with care.

T. flexuosa
Availability: rare   Size: large   Sunlight: A

This green-leaved variety is distinguished by the way it forms pups at the end of its flower stem (vivipara form). A robust variety, its leaves are wide and rigid and it recovers easily from dehydration. It grows well during its growth period from spring to summer, but is extremely vulnerable to cold. If the minimum temperature is less than 59F/15C degrees, keep it indoors and cut back on watering.

T. heteromorpha
Availability: rare   Size: medium   Sunlight: A

Individual plants of this silver-leaved variety can differ markedly. A caulescent variety that closely resembles *funckiana* (p73), this plant's leaves are slightly fleshier. It is easy to cultivate but is an extremely slow grower. In summer, keep it out of hot, humid places and make sure it is well aired.

T. "Peru Inca Gold"
Availability: rare   Size: medium   Sunlight: A

This green-leaved variety is distinguished by its slightly rigid leaves that curl inwards vertically. The leaves are extremely attractive, but are prone to snapping, so attach the plant to cork or some other board. It is easy to cultivate, and the fleshy leaves can be maintained by misting until the plant is dripping, showering the plant with water during its growth period and so on. Its flowers have a fragrance.

T. bergeri hybrid
Availability: rare   Size: large   Sunlight: A

A hybrid variety of the robust *bergeri*, shown in a clump in the photo. It is a green-leaved variety with a high tolerance for cold that can be cultivated outside all year round. Indoors, next to a window where there is plenty of light and the air is refreshed daily is an ideal spot. Extreme dryness causes the plant to wither, but with appropriate care it can be revived. It has light blue flowers when it is relatively cold.

T. hondurensis
Availability: rare   Size: large   Sunlight: A

This attractive variety has silver leaves covered in short trichomes. The leaves are fleshy, wide and slightly rigid. In order for the plant to grow large and sturdy, it is best to keep it outside during its growth period from spring to summer in a spot out of direct sunlight that is well ventilated.

T. macbrideana
Availability: rare   Size: medium   Sunlight: A

A caulescent variety with fine, soft, attractive silver leaves. In summer it molders and rots easily in high temperatures and humid conditions, so keep it somewhere cool where air circulates well. If many of its surfaces are in direct contact with objects it is easily damaged, so attach it to something like a cork board and hang it up to maintain its attractive appearance.

T. mallemontii
Availability: rare   Size: small   Sunlight: A

Although it resembles *usneoides* (p57), this silver-leaved variety has finer, more delicate leaves. The photograph shows an example with flower stems. The plant branches out in order to multiply. It is vulnerable to dryness so regular misting and good ventilation are important. It has pale purple flowers with a delightful fragrance.

T. myosura
Availability: rare   Size: small   Sunlight: A

This silver-leaved type has rigid leaves that grow in an alternating pattern, creating an individualistic look. In spring and summer it grows vigorously and forms pups readily, so should be attached to driftwood and the like in order to be hung in the air. It does not cope well with heat or steamy conditions, so keep it in a semi-shaded spot that is well ventilated in summer and never leave it in an enclosed space.

T. minasgeraisensis
Availability: rare   Size: medium   Sunlight: A

An attractive silver-leaved variety, it is relatively tough, grows to a large size and clumps readily. Its slightly fleshy leaves are easily damaged, so attaching it to a cork board or something similar makes it easier to maintain its attractive appearance than placing it on a surface as-is.

T. mima var. chilitensis
Availability: rare   Size: medium   Sunlight: A

The *mima* has widely spreading, boldly curling leaves. This silver-leaved variety has inherited these traits and grows in a superb rosette shape. As it is a vigorously growing type that likes water, it can also be cultivated in a pot with bark chips, pumice stones and so on for soil.

T. mollis
Availability: rare   Size: small   Sunlight: A

This variety has beautiful silver leaves and is known as a relative of *usneoides* (p57), although it has slightly fleshier, rigid leaves. Its growth is slow, but it is hardy and tolerates heat and cold well, making cultivation easy. It is best to grow it attached to driftwood, tree fern slab or something similar that is hanging in the air.

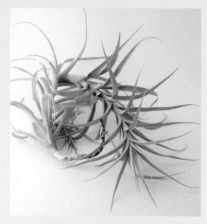

T. latifolia "Caulescent Form"
Availability: rare   Size: large   Sunlight: A

A caulescent form of the many *latifolia* hybrid varieties, this green-leaved variety is hardy and tolerates cold extremely well. If water is left to collect at the base of its leaves in winter it can get cold and is prone to rot, so reduce the frequency of watering in the cooler months and use a humidifier to raise the moisture levels in the air. Hang it in the air to prevent the leaves being damaged and to maintain its appearance.

T. latifolia "Small Form"
Availability: rare   Size: small   Sunlight: A

Among the *latifolia*, this green-leaved variety is unusual as it does not grow to a large size. It grows well if allowed to take root by being attached to something. It is fairly susceptible to moldering, so after watering make sure it is well aired and do not allow it to remain wet.

T. recurvifolia
Availability: rare   Size: medium   Sunlight: A

This beautiful silver-leaved variety is distinguished by its soft, fleshy leaves. Although it quite likes water, it is extremely prone to moldering in summer. Make sure to get rid of any excess water after watering and keep it in a spot where air circulates well.

T. recurvifolia subsecundifolia

Availability: rare   Size: medium   Sunlight: A

A hybrid of *recurvifolia* (above right), this variety has attractive silver leaves. It is a hardy variety that copes well with dry conditions, forms pups readily and is very easy to cultivate. Individual plants vary markedly.

T. roseoscapa

Availability: rare   Size: large   Sunlight: A

This silver-leaved caulescent variety grows to a giant size. Its rigid, fleshy leaves radiate out from its center. As it likes light, it can be kept outside from spring to summer, with the attractiveness of its leaves maintained as it becomes accustomed to the brightness. The tips of the leaves shrivel in low temperatures, so in winter reduce the frequency of watering a little. A humidifier is another effective maintenance measure.

T. loliacea

Availability: average   Size: small   Sunlight: A

A green-leaved dwarf variety that is easy to cultivate, readily forms pups and clumps easily. It has pretty yellow flowers. If it dries out, the plant can easily wither, so place it on top of western orchid bark or sphagnum moss. Keep it in a bright spot with natural light, making sure to avoid the strong western sun in summer.

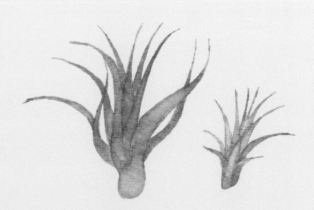

Index

Published by Tuttle Publishing, an imprint of Periplus Editions (HK) Ltd.

www.tuttlepublishing.com

Hajimete no Air Plants Sodatekata Kazarikata
Copyright © Yoshiharu Kashima 2016
Design: Kana Tsukada (ME & MIRACO)
Photography: Satomi Ochiai
Editing: Masayo Takishita
Illustrations: Michi Imai
Editorial services: Hiroko Sato
DTP Production: Tenryusya

Reference sources:
Air Plant Life (Nitto Shoin)
Fujikawa Tadao no Tillandsia Book (My Navi)

English translation rights arranged with
IE-NO-HIKARI-ASSOCIATION through
Japan UNI Agency, Inc., Tokyo
Translated from Japanese by Leeyong Soo
English Translation © 2018 by Periplus Editions (HK) Ltd.

ISBN: 978-0-8048-5104-6

Distributed by:

North America, Latin America & Europe
Tuttle Publishing
364 Innovation Drive, North Clarendon
VT 05759-9436 U.S.A.
Tel: 1 (802) 773-8930; Fax: 1 (802) 773-6993
info@tuttlepublishing.com; www.tuttlepublishing.com

Japan
Tuttle Publishing
Yaekari Building 3rd Floor
5-4-12 Osaki, Shinagawa-ku, Tokyo 141 0032
Tel: (81) 3 5437-0171; Fax: (81) 3 5437-0755
sales@tuttle.co.jp; www.tuttle.co.jp

Asia Pacific
Berkeley Books Pte. Ltd.
3 Kallang Sector, #04-01
Singapore 349278
Tel: (65) 6741-2178; Fax: (65) 6741-2179
inquiries@periplus.com.sg
www.tuttlepublishing.com

Printed in Hong Kong   1911EP
21 20 19   10 9 8 7 6 5 4 3 2

TUTTLE PUBLISHING® is a registered trademark of Tuttle Publishing, a division of Periplus Editions (HK) Ltd.

The Tuttle Story: "Books to Span the East and West"

Our core mission at Tuttle Publishing is to create books which bring people together one page at a time. Tuttle was founded in 1832 in the small New England town of Rutland, Vermont (USA). Our fundamental values remain as strong today as they were then—to publish best-in-class books informing the English-speaking world about the countries and peoples of Asia. The world has become a smaller place today and Asia's economic, cultural and political influence has expanded, yet the need for meaningful dialogue and information about this diverse region has never been greater. Since 1948, Tuttle has been a leader in publishing books on the cultures, arts, cuisines, languages and literatures of Asia. Our authors and photographers have won numerous awards and Tuttle has published thousands of books on subjects ranging from martial arts to paper crafts. We welcome you to explore the wealth of information available on Asia at **www.tuttlepublishing.com.**